Budgeting Your Time and Money

SOUTH-WESTERN

BUDGETING YOUR TIME & MONEY

Ransbottom & Nichol

LuEllen Ransbottom
Former Instructor
Adult and Vocational Education
Ormond Beach, Florida

Fran Moreland Nichol
Freelance Writer
Decatur, Georgia

SOUTH-WESTERN PUBLISHING CO.

Developmental Editor: *Mark Linton*
Senior Production Editor: *Alan Biondi*
Associate Director/Design: *Darren Wright*
Associate Photo Editor/Stylist: *Linda Ellis*
Marketing Manager: *Shelly Battenfield*

ISBN: 0-538-70838-7

1 2 3 4 5 6 7 8 H 99 98 97 96 95 94 93 92

Printed in the United States of America

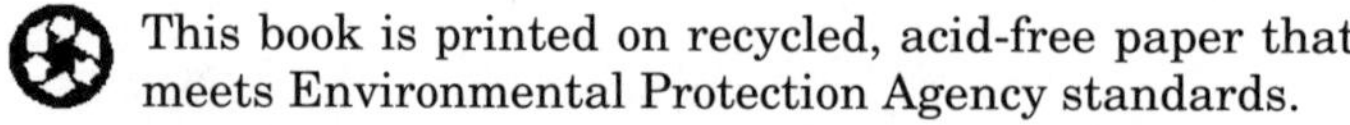

PREFACE

Budgeting Your Time and Money gives basic information on developing time and money management skills. This text-workbook is written specifically for the adult learner and is designed to permit self-paced, individualized instruction and foster student success.

The main focus of ***Budgeting Your Time and Money*** is on identifying ways to manage income and reduce expenses. Students learn practical ways to plan for making the best use of their time and money. There are also discussions of how to avoid financial troubles, and how to get out of financial troubles that may already be present.

SPECIAL FEATURES

Budgeting Your Time and Money is designed to help adult learners begin right now to manage time and money more effectively. Some features of the text-workbook include:

- A larger typeface is used to make the text-workbook easier for the student to read and use. Pages are colorful and uncrowded.
- Competency-based methodology is used. Clear objectives are presented followed by short segments of instruction. These are followed by student activities for immediate reinforcement.
- Content and examples relate to adult-level, real-life issues and skills.
- Pre- and post-tests, with answers and evaluation charts, are included for self-evaluation.
- Study breaks are included to provide refreshing and useful information that contributes to the general literacy of the student.
- Abundant exercises are included, each designed so that the student experiences frequent and meaningful success.
- Goals are listed for each exercise to provide motivation and direction.
- All exercises are supported with Bonus Exercises for the student who needs a second chance to succeed.
- Answers to all exercises are included to facilitate independent, self-paced learning.

- Personal progress is recorded by the student after completing each exercise.
- Individual success is measured by evaluation guides in the student's Personal Progress Record.

INSTRUCTOR'S MANUAL

The Instructor's Manual provides instructional strategies and specific teaching suggestions for ***Budgeting Your Time and Money,*** along with supplementary bonus exercises and answers, additional testing materials, and a certificate of completion.

Bonus Exercises. A bonus exercise, matching each exercise in the text-workbook, is provided in the manual. These bonus exercises make it possible for students to have a second chance to reach the goals set for each exercise. Answers to the bonus exercises are also provided in the manual. These materials may be reproduced for classroom use.

Testing Materials. Two additional tests, with answers, are provided in the manual to allow for more flexible instruction and evaluation.

Certificate of Completion. Upon completion of ***Budgeting Your Time and Money,*** a student's success may be recognized through a certificate of completion. This certificate lists the skills and topics covered in this text-workbook. A certificate master is included in the manual.

CONTENTS

GETTING ACQUAINTED

Have you ever had trouble making ends meet? Do you feel there is never quite enough time or money to go around? There are some good ways you can change all that. You will find them in this book.

You will learn to make the best use of your time and money. You will learn to budget your money, to reduce your costs, and plan your time. You will also learn ways to stay out of financial trouble, and ways to get out of trouble if it is already here.

HOW YOU WILL LEARN

Budgeting Your Time and Money is written with you in mind. You will learn the skills to help you start making your life better right away. This book begins with simple explanations of income and expense and takes you through steps you can practice to develop time- and money-saving skills.

Learn at Your Own Pace

You will progress through the lessons in this book at your own pace. You may move ahead faster, or go slower, than other students. But don't be concerned about this. You are to work at *your* best speed.

Learn Skills Successfully

You are given objectives and goals for each unit. You will know what you are to accomplish. You will study a topic. Then you will complete an exercise. This lets you drill over what you have just learned. When you have shown that you know the topic, you will move on to the next topic. You will always know just how well you are doing as you move through each step in this book.

Complete Bonus Exercises

You may not reach your goal on every practice exercise. When this happens, you should review the lesson and then complete a Bonus Exercise. These exercises cover the same lessons as the practice exercises in this book. They give you a second chance to reach your goal. When you score higher on a Bonus Exercise than you did on the original activity, you may change your score on your Personal Progress Record. Your instructor has copies of these Bonus Exercises and the answers to them.

Check Your Own Success

You will keep track of your own success. You will check all of your own work. The answers are in the back of this book. The color pages make them easy to find. Always do the exercises *before* you look at the answers. Use the answers as a tool to verify your work — not as a means of filling in the blanks. You will record your scores on your own Personal Progress Record, which is also in the back of this book.

WHAT YOU WILL LEARN

As you study this book, you will learn how to improve your skills for making the best use of time and money. These are skills that can help you every day.

In Unit 1, "Using A Budget," you will learn to identify sources of income, and to calculate monthly income and overtime pay. You will learn to identify different types of expenses. You will also learn how to prepare your own budget.

In Unit 2, "Cutting Costs," you will learn how to control your expenses and set reasonable limits. You will learn tips to help you cut costs

In Unit 3, "Saving Time and Money," you will learn some of the obstacles to saving time. You will learn how to set priorities and plan for the best use of your time. Maybe you are already in financial trouble. If so, this unit will help you learn ways to get out of trouble. You will also learn ways to stay out of financial trouble, and ways to begin saving money right away.

SPECIAL FEATURES

Budgeting Your Time and Money has a number of special features. These features will help you learn and apply the material successfully.

Checking What You Know

You can check what you already know about budgeting time and money before you start studying this book. Checking What You Know lets you know what skills you need to improve upon. Then, when you complete this book, you will do an exercise called *Checking What You Have Learned.* By comparing these two scores you will see how much you have gained through your study.

Making Your Money Work for You

This book has special features designed to give you a break from the regular study. These breaks have interesting stories about your money and helpful hints for making your money work for you.

Putting It Together

Each unit has a number of short exercises called *Checkpoints.* These exercises will help you check your understanding of a specific topic before continuing. At the end of each unit you will find a section titled *Putting It Together.* This section contains several exercises that are similar to the Checkpoints. They will help you to reinforce the skills you learned in each unit.

Personal Progress Record

You will keep track of your own progress. Once you check your answers, you will record your score on your Personal Progress Record at the end of this book. After you finish a unit, you will be able to see your level of success.

Completion Certificate

When you finish your study in this book, you may be eligible for a certificate of completion. Your instructor will explain to you the skill level required for this award.

READY TO START

You are now ready to start improving your skills for making the best use of your time and money. You can start improving those skills right away.

As you learn to budget your time and money, you will find these skills help in other ways. A good plan will make your time go farther. A good budget will make your money go farther. And saving money today will make your future better.

Turn to page xiii and complete Checking What You Know. Check your answers with the answers on page 53. Then begin Unit 1, "Using A Budget."

LuEllen Ransbottom
Fran Moreland Nichol

CHECKING WHAT YOU KNOW

Take this pre-test before starting *Budgeting Your Time and Money*. The 20 questions will tell you how much you already know about budgeting. They will also tell you what you need to learn.

There is no time limit, so take your time. When you finish, check your answers. Give yourself 1 point for each correct answer. Record you score on your Personal Progress Record. After finishing the book, you will be able to see how much you learned.

DIRECTIONS: Each statement is either true or false. Write *T* (true) or *F* (false) in the space provided.

______ 1. Income is paid in exchange for goods or labor.

______ 2. Aid for Families with Dependent Children (AFDC) monies are paid by the government to low-income families with dependent children.

______ 3. To change a bi-weekly income amount to a monthly amount, multiply by four (4).

______ 4. Expenses can either be fixed or variable.

______ 5. A budget can help you match expected earnings with expenses.

______ 6. A daily log of expenses should include all money spent for lunches, movies, or snacks.

______ 7. A budget should not include variable expenses.

______ 8. Sellers and advertisers do not count on impulse buyers to boost sales.

______ 9. Your water heater should be set at no more than 120 degrees.

______ 10. Open draperies on sunny days during winter months save energy.

______ 11. Operator-assisted long-distance calls are cheaper than dialing direct.

______ 12. Buying by unit pricing can save on grocery bills.

______ 13. Looking at several brands of items and their prices before you buy is called impulse shopping.

______ 14. Fixed expenses are ones you can control.

_____ 15. To save time, stand up when you talk on the telephone.

_____ 16. Setting priorities cannot help you save time or money.

_____ 17. One category to list on a priority chart is Financial.

_____ 18. Consumer Credit Counseling Services offers free counseling to help you get out of debt.

_____ 19. When using a savings account, the principal is the money that you deposit into the account.

_____ 20. A passbook savings account cannot be opened with a small amount of money.

☞ ***Check Your work on page 53. Record your score on page 57.***

UNIT 1

Using a Budget

WHAT YOU WILL LEARN

When you finish this unit, you will be able to:

- List all of your income.
- List your expenses.
- Prepare a monthly budget.

Meet Rose Anna Valentine. For Rose Anna, life has never been very easy. She is beginning to do better, though. How? How can anyone have more money? A good way to have more money, as pictured in Illustration 1-1, is through money management.

When Rose Anna was growing up she shared a crowded room with her sisters. She used to make a little money babysitting. But it didn't go far. Usually she didn't remember how she had spent it.

Rose Anna dropped out of school in the ninth grade. She had a pretty good job at the discount store. She thought she could get along. She and Tony got married when they were both 17. Things were okay for a while, but bills kept piling up. Finally, they separated, and Tony took a job in another city.

Now Rose Anna shares a room with her kids. Buster is six and goes to school and day care. Tisha is still in diapers. Rose Anna's mother keeps Tisha while Rose Anna works at the discount store. Rose Anna has gotten two pay raises, and Tony sends child support. But there is still never enough money.

Rose Anna is going through this book with you. By the time you finish, she will be managing her life and her money better. You will, too!

Illustration 1-1

A good way to have more money is through money management.

INCOME

Do you wish you had more money? Most of us do. How can you have more money? One way is by managing your money so that more is coming in than going out each month.

Income is the amount of money that is paid to you during a period of time. Income is paid in exchange for labor or services. Income can also come from the sale of goods or property. Other sources of income are discussed next.

Sources of Income

Income comes from several sources. A regular paycheck once a week, every two weeks, or once a month is the most common. A paycheck is shown in Illustration 1-2.

Look at the *check stub* on the right side of Rose Anna's check. She earns $220.00 per week. This total amount is her gross pay. **Gross pay** is the total amount of earnings for a specified period of time such as one month, two weeks, or one week. **Gross pay** is the total amount of earnings for a specified period of time such as one month, two weeks, or one week. Social security taxes (FICA) are taken out of (*deducted from*) the total earnings. Rose Anna does not have any federal taxes deducted. That is because she supports Buster and Tisha and does not make very much money.

DMi Discount Mart, Inc.
2602 E. 10th Street • Ormond Beach, FL 32174-2612

56-680
422

NO. 2853

DATE MONTH 5 DAY 16 YEAR --

PAY TO THE ORDER OF Rose Anna Valentine $ 203|17

FOR CLASSROOM USE ONLY

Discount Mart, Inc.

ENTERPRISE NATIONAL BANK
Ormond Beach, FL 32174-2265

Anne K. Rollins
AUTHORIZED SIGNATURE

⑆0422068041⑆ 2163⑈1026⑈

DETACH BEFORE CASHING

DATE 5 | 16 | --
NO. 2853

GROSS PAY 220.00

DEDUCTIONS
FICA 16.83
Fed. W.T.

NET PAY 203.17

Discount Mart, Inc.
Ormand Beach, FL 32174-2612

Illustration 1-2

Rose Anna's Paycheck

Rose Anna receives *net pay* of $203.17 every week. **Net pay** is what is left after all the deductions are taken out of the paycheck, or from gross pay.

Child support is money paid by one parent to the other for support of dependent children. **Aid to Families with Dependent Children** (AFDC) is money paid by the federal government to low-income families with dependent children.

Food stamps can add to your income, also. Not everyone qualifies to receive food stamps. Income and number of dependents determines whether you qualify for food stamps. A **dependent** is someone who relies on another for support. Dependents are usually children, but may include elderly parents or other family members you support. These food stamps are given out by a department in each state. Usually the department is called *Health and Rehabilitative Services (HRS)*, or *Department of Human Services (DHS)*, or a similar name. Check for the department under *state government* in your telephone book.

Part-time work, or overtime every now and then, are other sources of income. Or income may come from: pension payments, social security payments, welfare payments, or other government programs.

Calculating Monthly Income and Overtime Pay

Some paychecks are given out weekly. Other paychecks are given out every two weeks (biweekly.) Some paychecks are given out monthly. Weekly or biweekly paychecks are the most common. But managing your income and expenses is easier when all figures are in monthly amounts.

To change weekly paycheck amounts to monthly income, multiply by four. For example, Rose Anna receives $203.17 each week. Four weeks are in a month.

$203.17	a week
x 4	weeks
$812.68	a month

To change biweekly paycheck amounts to monthly income, multiply by two. For example, Rose Anna's friend, Chikara, earns $500 every two weeks. He is paid two times a month.

$ 500	every two weeks
x 2	
$1,000	a month

Overtime is paid at the rate of one and one-half times the hourly rate. For example, Carmen earns $6.40 an hour working at a poultry processing plant. Overtime pay is $9.60 an hour. If Carmen works five hours of overtime, she earns $48 extra pay.

$ 9.60	overtime rate
x 5	hours worked overtime
$48.00	overtime pay

Rose Anna listed her income for one month. She was surprised to see how much she would earn this month. Rose Anna's list is shown in Illustration 1-3, below.

Illustration 1-3

Rose Anna's Income

Income

Take Home Pay from Regular Job	$ 812.68
Take Home Pay from Part-Time Job	30.80
Income from other sources	125.00
Grand Total Monthly Income.	$ 968.48

CHECKPOINT 1-1

YOUR GOAL: Get 2 or more points.

List your sources of monthly income in the spaces provided. Write the amounts received from those sources in the spaces provided. Add the amounts of income to find a total monthly income. An example is done for you.

Sources of Income	Amounts
• **Paycheck**	**($150, two times a month)**
1. ________	$ ________
2. ________	________
3. ________	________
4. ________	________
5. Total monthly income	$ ________

☞ *Check your work on page 53. Record your score on page 58.*

EXPENSES

Expenses are payments for goods and services. For example, the telephone bill, water and sewer bill, your home gas and electric bill, gasoline for your car, food, haircuts, rent or mortgage payments, insurance premium payments, and clothing are expenses. Expenses can be fixed or variable.

MAKING YOUR MONEY WORK FOR YOU

Remember how Grandmother used to say, “Pennies make dimes, dimes make dollars”? It's true! Ask anyone at a nearby bank to give you some papers for rolling pennies and dimes. Then empty your pockets or purse every night for two weeks. Put the pennies into one cup; the dimes into another cup. See how quickly you have enough to make a full roll. And you probably won't miss those pennies and dimes in the morning.

Fixed Expenses

Fixed expenses are those expenses that are the same amount each month. Examples are savings, house payments, utilities, car payments, insurance premiums, and average gasoline and car maintenance costs. A list of fixed expenses is shown next, in Illustration 1-4.

Illustration 1-4

Rose Anna's Fixed Expenses

Fixed Expenses

Rent	$ 300.00
Bus fare to work	25.00
Utilities	65.00
Child care (Buster after school) . . .	40.00
Child care (payment to Grandmother for Tisha's food, diapers, etc.)	60.00
Savings	20.00
Total Fixed Expenses. . .	$ 510.00

CHECKPOINT 1-2

YOUR GOAL: Get 2 or more points.

List your fixed expenses for one month in the spaces provided. Write the amount of each fixed expense in the space provided. Add the amounts of your fixed expenses to find a total amount of fixed expenses for one month. An example is done for you.

Fixed Expenses	Amounts
• **Life insurance premium**	**$ 17.50**
1. ________________	________
2. ________________	________

Fixed Expenses	Amounts
3. ______________________	$ ________
4. ______________________	________
5. Total Fixed Expenses	$ ________

☞ ***Check your work on page 53. Record your score on page 58.***

Variable Expenses

Variable expenses are expenses that vary from day to day. Usually, the change is very small. But money should be available to cover these expenses. Examples of variable expenses are telephone, groceries, dental or medical bills, entertainment expenses, recreation, and miscellaneous purchases. Some variable expenses are listed in Illustration 1-5.

Illustration 1-5

Rose Anna's Variable Expenses

Variable Expenses

Groceries	$ 210.00
Lunches Out	40.00
Laundry	20.00
Telephone (includes long distance)	35.00
Doctor--Tisha's shots	35.00
Buster's school supplies	7.00
Haircut	12.00
Clothing (for 3)	60.00
Entertainment (movies & pizza)	30.00
Miscellaneous	9.48
Total flexible Exp.	$458.48

CHECKPOINT 1-3

YOUR GOAL: Get 2 or more points.

List your variable expenses in the spaces provided. Write the amount of each variable expense in the space provided. Add all amounts to find the total amount of your variable expenses for one month. An example is done for you.

	Variable Expenses	Amounts
•	**Groceries**	$ **275**
1.		$
2.		$
3.		$
4.		$
5.		$
6.	Total Variable Expenses	$

☞ *Check your work on page 53. Record your score on page 58.*

Keeping a Daily Log of Expenses

To prepare a realistic budget (studied next), you must track your expenses. You need to know where your money is going. When you know where your money is going, you can make a plan to manage it.

Carry a small notebook in your purse or pocket. Write down *everything* you spend, *every time* you spend it. Write down every

MAKING YOUR MONEY WORK FOR YOU

Here is a way Rose Anna found she could make her savings grow: For one week, she spent $2 less on each of her variable expenses. You can, too! Pick one week in the month. Spend just $2 less on each of your variable expenses for that week. The next month, you may want to spend $3 less on each variable expense!

penny. After a few weeks, you will see where your money is going. You will see that you spend more than what you have listed as fixed and variable expenses. You will be surprised at what you buy each month. You will see ways to cut expenses.

If you don't have a notebook, make a daily log on a plain piece of paper. Fold an 8-1/2" x 11" piece of paper into eight parts as shown in Illustration 1-6. Open the folded paper and mark seven sections for each day of the week. The eighth section is for your weekly totals.

To keep track of your expenses for one month, make four folded pieces of paper. You will have the information you need for preparing your budget.

Rose Anna kept a daily log for one week. She was surprised to see how much she spent on lunches at work. She saw other ways she had spent money she might have saved. Illustration 1-6 shows the kind of daily log Rose Anna made.

Mon.	Tues.	Wed.	Thurs.
Bus tokens $6.00	Personal items $3.00 Book for Buster 6.00	Groceries $12.00 Lunch at work 3.00	Personal items $4.00
Fri.	**Sat.**	**Sun.**	**Totals**
Notebook for Buster $3.50	Groceries $42.00 Laundry 12.00 Movie 7.00	Pizza $3.00	Bus tokens $6.00 Personal items 7.00 School supplies 9.50 Lunch 3.00 Groceries 54.00 Laundry 12.00 Entertainment 7.00 Other food 3.50

Illustration 1-6

Rose Anna's Daily Log

CHECKPOINT 1-4

YOUR GOAL: Get 6 or more points.

Make a daily log for yourself for one week. Use a plain piece of paper. Fold the paper and label the sections as was shown in Illustration 1-6 on the previous page.

☞ ***Check your work on page 53. Record your score on page 58.***

MONTHLY BUDGET

A **budget** is a written plan to help you live within your income. A budget will not get you more money, but it can make your money go farther. Because most regular bills are monthly bills, most budgets are for one month. A budget will help you:

- Match your expected income to your expenses.
- Avoid buying things you don't really need.
- Make wise choices in the things you buy.
- Save for the future.

Now that you have seen where your money is going, you can prepare a full budget plan. You will need to combine your income and expenses on one form. You need to see the whole picture. For example, Rose Anna kept her daily log for three more weeks. Then she could see the whole month. She wanted to buy a winter coat. Her budget includes weekly savings toward buying a new coat, as shown in Illustration 1-7.

Income

Take Home Pay from Regular Job	$ 812.68
Take Home Pay from Part-Time Job	30.80
Income from Other Sources (child support $120.00 baby-sitting 5.00)	125.00
Grand Total Monthly Income	$ 968.48

Expenses

Fixed Expenses		Variable Expenses	
Rent	$300.00	Groceries	$210.00
Bus fare to work	25.00	Lunches out	40.00
Utilities	65.00	Laundry	20.00
Child care (Buster after school)	40.00	Telephone (Including Long Distance)	35.00
Child care Payment to grandmother for Tisha's food, diapers, etc.)	60.00	Doctor—Tisha's shots	35.00
		Buster's school supplies	7.00
		Haircut	12.00
		Clothing (for 3)	60.00
Savings	20.00	Entertainment (movie, pizza)	30.00
		Miscellaneous	9.48
Total Fixed Exp.	$510.00	Total Flexible Exp.	$458.48

Total Fixed Expenses	$510.00
Total Variable Expenses	458.48
Total Expenses	$968.48

Illustration 1-7

Rose Anna's Monthly Budget

WHAT YOU HAVE LEARNED

After studying this unit, you have learned:

- What your total monthly income is.
- Where your money is going.
- What your fixed and variable expenses are.
- Where you are spending too much money.
- How to prepare a monthly budget to plan for the things you want.

PUTTING IT TOGETHER

ACTIVITY 1-1 **YOUR GOAL:** Get 10 or more points.

Prepare a monthly budget. Fill in your income and expenses in the space provided below.

INCOME

Take Home Pay from Regular Job .... $ ____________

Take Home Pay from Part-Time Job .... $ ____________

Income from Other Sources .... $ ____________

EXPENSES

FIXED EXPENSES		VARIABLE EXPENSES	
____________	$ ______	____________	$ ______
____________	$ ______	____________	$ ______
____________	$ ______	____________	$ ______
____________	$ ______	____________	$ ______
____________	$ ______	____________	$ ______
____________	$ ______	____________	$ ______
____________	$ ______	____________	$ ______
____________	$ ______	____________	$ ______
____________	$ ______	____________	$ ______
Total Fixed Exp. . .	$ ______	Total Flexible Exp.	$ ______

Total Fixed Expenses .... $ ____________

Total Variable Expenses ..... $ ____________

TOTAL EXPENSES .... $ ____________

GRAND TOTAL MONTHLY INCOME . . . . $ ____________

☞ ***Check your work on page 53. Record your score on page 58.***

ACTIVITY 1-2 YOUR GOAL: Get 6 or more points.

Help Marion complete a daily log. Marion's daily expenses are listed below. Fill in the expenses for each day on the daily log. Then add the totals and write them in the last box. Compare the totals with Marion's budget listed below. Circle each total in the last box where Marion spent too much.

<u>Monday</u>

Groceries: $20

Lunch: $10

<u>Tuesday</u>

Personal items: $10

Lunch: $10

Movies: $14

<u>Wednesday</u>

Lunch: $10

<u>Thursday</u>

Groceries: $40

Lunch: $5

Movies: $14

<u>Friday</u>

Personal items: $16

Lunch: $10

Clothing: $5

<u>Saturday</u>

Groceries: $10

Clothing: $10

Movies: $7

<u>Sunday</u>

Personal items: $5

Marion's budget included the following:

Groceries: $60

Personal items: $16

Clothing: $30

Lunches: $25

Movies: $14

Monday	***Tuesday***	***Wednesday***	***Thursday***
Friday	***Saturday***	***Sunday***	***TOTALS***

☞ ***Check your work on page 53. Record your score on page 58.***

UNIT 2 Cutting Costs

WHAT YOU WILL LEARN

When you finish this unit, you will be able to:

- List five questions to ask yourself before you spend.
- List five rules to follow in cutting costs.
- Set reasonable limits for living expenses.
- List five cost-cutting tips for everyday use.

Buster really wanted a new shirt. "All the other guys have new shirts," he told his mother. "They have their names written on the front."

"We have spent all of our clothing budget for this month already," Rose Anna said. "But maybe we can think of something. Bring me that shirt Grandmother gave you for Christmas. We can put iron-on letters on it. That will be even better than the other ones!"

While they fixed the shirt, Rose Anna and Buster talked about other ways they could cut costs. In this unit are some steps you can take to cut costs, too

CONTROLLING VARIABLE EXPENSES

Variable expenses can be controlled. The first step in cutting costs is to look at your variable expenses and find ways to make them go down.

Questions to Ask Yourself before You Spend

Rose Anna and Buster began making a list of questions to ask themselves. Some of the questions they listed are:

1. Do I really need it?
2. Can I buy it later, maybe when it is on sale?
3. Can I buy it somewhere else, such as a second hand or discount store, for less?
4. Can I make it myself and save money?
5. Can I postpone buying it and save the extra money I would end up spending if I bought it on credit?
6. Can I postpone buying it for one week and see if I still want or need it then?
7. Am I being taken in by advertising? Do I want this item because I've seen it advertised on TV?

Asking these questions before you buy will help you avoid impulse buying. **Impulse buying** is spending money suddenly (on an impulse) for something because you think you want it. As pictured in Illustration 2-1, we can all be confused about whether we actually need some things. Sellers and advertisers count on impulse buyers to boost sales. But you can learn to resist impulse buying.

Rose Anna promised she would ask herself questions before she bought. Buster agreed that he would ask the same questions about things he wanted. Learning how to avoid impulse buying is a valuable lesson for children as well as adults.

MAKING YOUR MONEY WORK FOR YOU

One answer to impulse buying is Wrong Time Buying. Try buying the things you need at times you don't need them. Often, you can save money this way. How does Wrong Time Buying work? Buy sweaters or blankets in the springtime or early summer; buy Christmas wrapping paper in January or a bathing suit in September. Retailers often offer the best prices just before they have to put goods away for an expensive storage period.

Rules to Follow for Cost-Cutting

Besides asking questions before you spend, there are rules to follow for controlling your variable expenses. Following these rules will help you spend less.

Illustration 2-1

Impulse buying is spending money suddenly for something because you think you want it.

Then, when you get back home, you wonder why you bought it.

1. ***Don't Buy It.*** Sometimes this is an easy rule. If you answer no to the question, Do I really need it?, or answer yes to the question, Can I buy it later? then follow this rule: Don't buy it.
2. ***Shop Around and Compare.*** Look in more than one place for the best price. Shopping around also means watching ads and prices for the best day to buy. Watch for sales. Compare prices. Buying goods out of season can help you cut costs.
3. ***Do It Yourself.*** Often you can save by making something yourself, if you have the skills. Another good way to save is by buying used goods and refinishing or remaking them. A second-hand coat with a new collar may work for you. Or a used chair with a new coat of paint may give you what you need at a fraction of the cost.
4. ***Substitute.*** Look for something else that will work just as well. Often you will find something better for less.
5. ***Trade.*** If you have baby furniture you no longer need, trade it to a neighbor who has extra tableware you could use. Or you may be able to trade a skill, such as babysitting, carpentry, or house cleaning.
6. ***Ask Questions.*** Don't believe everything the ads say. Ask questions about how well a product will work and how long it will last.
7. ***Share.*** Go together with family and friends to buy cheaper in bulk (larger quantity). Share little-used tools, magazines, and other items to make one purchase useful to several people.
8. ***Watch Your Mood.*** Don't shop when you are sad or angry. Never go to the grocery store when you are hungry.

9. ***Plan.*** Know your needs ahead of time and stick to your buying plan. Don't be talked into buying something you don't need.
10. ***Use Wisely.*** Many expenses can be cut simply by being careful with the way you use goods. Store foods quickly and properly. Notice expiration dates and use foods before the expiration date. Keep clothes and closets clean; clothes will last longer. Fix water leaks quickly. Keep heat vents clean and fix drafty places that may be making your bills go up. You can make your own list to add to this rule.

CHECKPOINT 2-1

YOUR GOAL: Get 4 or more points.

Carefully read each statement. Each statement is either true or false. Write *T* beside each true statement, or *F* beside each false statement, in the space provided. An example is done for you.

__T__ • You can save money by trading your skills for something you need.

____ 1. Impulse buying is a useful plan.

____ 2. Buying goods out of season can help you cut costs.

____ 3. Watching ads can help you find goods on sale.

____ 4. Careful use of goods and equipment does not help cut costs.

____ 5. A good question to ask before buying is, Can I buy it later?

____ 6. Shopping two places for one item is a waste of time.

☞ ***Check your work on page 54. Record your score on page 58.***

SETTING REASONABLE LIMITS

You may wonder how your spending compares with others'. Rose Anna had the same question. Rose Anna knew her budget limits. But she wondered if she were spending too much on one part of her budget or another.

Your spending limits will change from year to year. You may spend more on education if you go back to school. Or you may spend less on medical bills if the whole family stays well. But you can set reasonable limits. For the average family just beginning to manage its money, the ranges in Illustration 2-2 will usually apply.

Illustration 2-2

Family Spending

Budget Category	Percentage of Take-Home Pay
Housing (Including rent, and utilities)	20 - 30%
Food	20 - 30%
Clothing	5 - 10%
Transportation	10 - 20%
Personal	2 - 5%
Medical	3 - 10%
Savings	0 - 10%
Education & Recreation	0 - 10%
Miscellaneous	2 - 10%

The ranges in Illustration 2-2 are shown as percentages. Percentages are fractions using 100 to represent the whole. Another way to show percentages is to write them as decimal amounts. For example,

25% = .25 or 5% = .05 or 75% = .75

A decimal amount is a number using a decimal point (period) to show the percentage. To calculate percentages, write them as decimal amounts and multiply by your total. For example,

To calculate 25% of $4,000, multiply $4,000 by .25; $4,000 x .25 = $1,000.

Where you fall in the budget categories will depend on several things:

1. The ages in your family. If you have growing children, you may need to spend more on clothing.
2. The health of your family. Caring for an elderly relative or sick child may increase your medical needs.

3. Your priorities. You may feel it is important to save for the future, to give money to church or charities, or to go to the movies every week.

All of these circumstances change. Making small changes or short-term changes will bring more success. You can cut costs by making small changes in your spending limits. Ask yourself these questions:

1. Can I lower this limit for six months? (For example, can I put off buying any new clothes, or use less expensive transportation for a while?)
2. Can I change my priorities by just a few dollars? (For example, can I reasonably budget $10 a month less for movies?)

CHECKPOINT 2-2

YOUR GOAL: Get 6 or more points.

The Johnson family is made up of George and Sara Johnson and their two children — Kathy, 12, and Karl, 6. George and Sara together have take-home pay of $2,400 a month. Calculate the amounts the Johnsons should spend on each category. Multiply each decimal amount (percentage) given by $2,400. Write the answer in the space provided. An example is done for you.

	Budget Category	Percentage	Amount
•	Housing	$2,400 x .25	*$600*
1.	Food	.25	______
2.	Clothing	.05	______
3.	Transportation	.10	______
4.	Personal	.05	______
5.	Medical	.10	______
6.	Savings	.05	______
7.	Education/Recreation	.10	______
8.	Miscellaneous	.05	______
	Total	**100%**	______

☞ ***Check your work on page 54. Record your score on page 58.***

TIPS TO HELP YOU CUT COSTS

Monthly bills for water, electricity, gas, and telephone can be reduced by making simple changes. Follow these rules to cut your household costs:

Water bills

1. Don't leave the water running while you brush your teeth.
2. Fix faucet leaks promptly.
3. Put a quart jar filled with water in the corner of each toilet tank. Be sure it is in a corner where it does not get in the way of the machinery. The jar of water takes up space that previously was filled with water. It cuts down on water use but does not affect operation of the toilet.
4. Put water saver heads on showers and faucets. They will pay for themselves within a few months.

Electric bills

1. Set your water heater thermostat to provide the temperature needed (120 degrees is usually high enough). If you are going to be gone more than two days, turn the water heater off.
2. Take showers instead of baths.
3. Use portable electric heaters as little as possible.
4. Turn off lights and TV sets when not needed.
5. Replace light bulbs with lower wattage bulbs.

Another way to control electricity costs is to know where the most electricity is used. Appliances that use the most and least amounts of electricity are listed below, in Illustration 2-3.

Illustration 2-3

Electricity Use by Appliances

Most Electricity Use	Least Electricity Use
Air conditioner	Sewing machine
Water heater	Mixer, blender
Frostfree refrigerator	Hair dryer
Clothes dryer	Vacuum cleaner
Range with oven	Fan, clock, radio

Gas bills

1. Set daytime temperature on home heating units at 65 degrees during the winter months. Don't make changes in the setting. If no one is at home during the day, set the control at 60 degrees until you come home.
2. Keep closet doors and doors to unused rooms closed.
3. Use cold or warm water instead of hot whenever possible.
4. Open draperies and raise shades to let sunshine in during winter months.
5. Keep all heating equipment in good condition.
6. Make sure pilot lights on stove and in oven stay on so they don't waste gas or possibly cause an explosion.

Telephone bills

1. Dial all long-distance calls direct.
2. Make long-distance calls when the rates are lowest:
   Between 11 p.m. and 8 a.m. daily
   All day Saturday
   Sunday from 8 a.m. to 5 p.m.
3. Buy your own telephone equipment to avoid monthly charges.
4. Avoid using Information (Directory Assistance) for local telephone calls. Look up local numbers in the telephone directory.

Food bills

1. Learn to use unit pricing. **Unit pricing** is showing the price of an item by one unit: by weight, quantity, piece, etc. For example, a box of cereal may be priced at $2.79. The unit price is 17.4 cents an ounce. A larger box may be priced at $3.65, but the unit price is 13.4 cents an ounce. The larger box is the better buy. Using unit pricing can help you get the most for your money.

Illustration 2-4

Using unit pricing can help you get the most for your money.

2. Save coupons. Manufacturers' coupons can save you money on the products you use. Some stores offer double coupons on certain days. Double coupon offers mean the store will give you double the amount on your manufacturer's coupon.

3. Shop with a plan. Make a list before you go to the store and buy only what is on the list.

4. Comparison shop. Get in the habit of comparing one store's prices with another. Look at several brands of items you need before you choose.

5. Cook by season. Plan your meals around foods that are in season and offered at special prices.

6. Limit your trips to the store. Make one trip do for the week. Avoid stopping for one or two items.

CHECKPOINT 2-3

YOUR GOAL: Get 4 or more points.

Read the statements carefully. Write the correct word or words to complete the sentences. Use words from the list below. An example is done for you.

- Long-distance calls are cheaper when you **dial direct.**

1. It is cheaper to wash clothes with ____________________.
2. One appliance that takes a great deal of electricity to run is the ____________________.
3. You can save money by limiting calls for ____________________.
4. Buying by ____________________ can save on grocery bills.
5. Water costs are often increased because of ____________________.
6. Setting the ____________________ lower in winter can save on heating bills.

cold water
clothes dryer
leaky faucets
unit price
dial direct
directory assistance
thermostat

☞ ***Check your work on page 54. Record your score on page 58.***

WHAT YOU HAVE LEARNED

After studying this unit, you have learned:

- Five questions to ask yourself before you spend.
- Five rules to follow in cutting costs.
- How to set reasonable limits for living expenses.
- Five cost-cutting tips for everyday use.

PUTTING IT TOGETHER

ACTIVITY 2-1 **YOUR GOAL:** Get 7 or more points.

For each spending occasion described below, choose one question you should ask yourself before you spend. Use the questions listed on page 18. Choose one rule to follow for cost-cutting from those listed on pages 19 and 20. Write your choices in the space provided. An example is done for you.

- While shopping in the drug store, you notice a large display of a new cologne.

  Question: ***Do I really need it?***

  Rule: ***If the answer is no, then don't buy it.***

1. Your child wants the latest fad in sneakers.

   Question: ______________________

   Rule: ______________________

2. Your radio is old and not getting clear reception. You find one you like, but you won't have the cash for two or three months.

   Question: ______________________

   Rule: ______________________

3. You see an ad in the paper for a radio. The ad indicates that the Suggested Retail Price is $400.00, but the store is selling it for only $139.95.

   Question: ______________________

   Rule: ______________________

4. The store just received its shipment of swim suits. You find one you like, but the price is higher than you expected to pay.

   Question: ______________________

   Rule: ______________________

5. You need a new chair for the dining table. You have some skills in refinishing wood.

   Question: ______________________________

   Rule: ______________________________

☞ *Check your work on page 54. Record your score on page 58.*

ACTIVITY 2-2 YOUR GOAL: Get 4 or more points.

Match the action taken to cut costs in the left column with the related bills in the right column. Write your answer in the space provided. An example is done for you.

Action Taken		Related Bills
d	• Repaired leaky faucet.	a. Electric Bills
_____	1. Turned off lights in unoccupied room.	b. Food Bills
_____	2. Made a list of needed items before shopping.	c. Gas Bills
_____	3. Looked up local number in book instead of calling directory assistance.	d. Water Bills
_____	4. Lowered water heater thermostat to 120 degrees.	e. Telephone Bills
_____	5. Used manufacturers' coupons for needed products.	
_____	6. Used cold water to wash clothes.	

☞ *Check your work on page 54. Record your score on page 58.*

ACTIVITY 2-3 YOUR GOAL: Get 3 or more points.

Read the information about the product in each group below. Compare the unit prices in each group. Choose the best buy in each group. Write your answer in the space provided. An example is done for you.

	Product	Size	Total Cost	Unit Price	Best Buy
● a.	orange juice	64 oz.	$2.74	4.28¢/oz.	a
b.	orange juice	32 oz.	$1.59	4.97¢/oz.	
1. a.	1 qt. milk	32 oz.	$0.85	2.75¢/oz.	______
b.	1/2 gal. milk	64 oz.	$1.49	2.32¢/oz.	
c.	1 gal. milk	128 oz.	$2.49	1.94¢/oz.	
2. a.	chicken, whole	3 lb.	$2.67	$0.89/lb.	______
b.	chicken, cut up	3 lb.	$3.27	$1.09/lb.	
3. a.	soft drink 2 ltr. bottle	67.6 oz. -	$1.09	1.61¢/oz.	______
b.	soft drink 6 pk. cans	72 oz.	$1.99	2.76¢/oz.	______
4. a.	steak, T-bone	2 lb.	$7.98	$3.99/lb.	______
b.	steak, round	2 lb.	$4.10	$2.05/lb.	
5. a.	frozen pizza	18 oz.	$1.99	11.06¢/oz.	______
b.	frozen pizza	6 3/4 oz.	$1.99	29.48¢/oz.	

☞ *Check your work on page 54. Record your score on page 58.*

UNIT 3 Saving Time and Money

WHAT YOU WILL LEARN

When you finish this unit, you will be able to:

- Identify obstacles to saving time.
- Set priorities for time use.
- Prepare a time use inventory.
- Identify steps to get out of financial trouble.
- Identify two ways to save for the future.

Rose Anna hung up the telephone. She had been talking to her friend Silvia for 15 minutes. "I am really behind," she said to herself. "I wanted to go shopping this morning and get that broken drawer fixed. Now it's almost lunch time, and I have not done a thing!"

Rose Anna decided to make some changes. She decided to find out how to use her time and money better. On the next few pages are some ways Rose Anna found to save time and money. Using the same guides, you can save time and money, too.

SAVING TIME

Before you can make the best use of your time, you must know where you are wasting time. Most of us waste time every day. Rose Anna did! She made a list of ways she wasted time so she could begin to change.

Obstacles to Saving Time

An **obstacle** is something that stands in your way. Some of the obstacles to using time wisely are listed below. Beside each one are ways you can turn obstacles into time-savers.

1. *Telephone calls.* Don't use the telephone for long visits. Say what you need to say and hang up. Stand up when you talk on the phone; you won't talk as long.
2. *Mail.* Handle mail only once. Put bills where you can pay them without looking for them. Don't let junk mail pile up for a time that you can read it. Throw it away.
3. *Clutter.* Clutter makes confusion. Keep your work area clear. Finish one job before starting another.
4. *Radio and TV.* Limit your TV time. If you are doing a job, keep the radio volume low so you won't be distracted.
5. *Putting things off.* Before you put off a project, ask yourself why you can't do it right away. A good rule to follow is *DO IT NOW.* That will save you time.
6. *Being too tired.* When you put things off, you often come back to them when you are too tired. Don't try to do all of your big jobs on one day. Distribute your work through the week so you won't be too tired at the end of the week.
7. *Doing jobs in the wrong order.* If you have three things to do, do the most difficult one first. The easy jobs will go faster. Divide big projects into small jobs, and do the most difficult part first.
8. *Failure to plan.* Make a list of activities you need to do. Keep the list in front of you. Use it as a guide. Make a note of the most important activities and do them first. Let your list guide you to work smarter, not harder.

CHECKPOINT 3-1

YOUR GOAL: Get 4 or more points.

Read the following six statements. Each statement is either True or False. Write *T* (True) or *F* (False) in the space provided. An example is done for you.

F • It is wise to do difficult jobs last.

_______ 1. Standing up while talking on the phone helps save time because you don't talk as long.

_______ 2. Reading junk mail carefully is a good idea.

Illustration 3-1

Decide now to find out how to make the best use of your time and money.

________3. A list of activities can help you save time.

________4. Clutter causes confusion and wastes time.

________5. Turning up the radio helps you work better and faster.

________6. A good rule to follow is *DO IT NOW*.

☞ ***Check your work on page 54. Record your score on page 58.***

Setting Priorities

Priorities are orders of importance. Setting priorities can help you save time and money. You can identify your priorities by making a priority chart. A priority chart lists the things that are most important for you to accomplish.

Five general categories of activities for a priority chart are:

Education

Job

Financial

Family/Social

Physical

Your priority chart may change at different times of your life. For example, education may take most of your time for a while. If you have been ill, the physical part of your life may take most of your time. If you are supporting a family, your job is probably the most important thing you do.

To make a priority chart, list the most important things for you to work on right now. One might be learning a new skill (Job). Another might be to help your child with homework (Family). Rose Anna's priority chart is shown next, in Illustration 3-2.

Priority Chart

Category	Activity
Job	Study manual for supervisor's position.
	Dress Professionally (clothes clean, pressed, mended).
Physical	Exercise 30 minutes, 4 times a week.
	Get 6 to 8 hours of sleep daily.
Financial	Keep daily expense log.
	Pay Bills once a week.
Family/Social	Read to Tisha at bedtime.
	Make new friends.
Education	Work with Buster on his homework.
	Take classes to earn High School Diploma.

Illustration 3-2

Rose Anna's Priority Chart

CHECKPOINT 3-2

YOUR GOAL: Get 8 or more points.

On the next page, prepare a priority chart for yourself. Under each of the five categories, list at least two activities that are important to you now. Write your answers in the spaces provided. A good example for everyone is listed under "Financial."

PRIORITY CHART

Category	**Activity**
Job	______________________
	______________________
Physical	______________________
	______________________
Financial	***Keep my daily expense log***
	______________________
Family/Social	______________________
	______________________
Education	______________________
	______________________

☞ ***Check your work on page 54. Record your score on page 58.***

Preparing a Time Use Inventory

The next step in saving time is to plan your day. Preparing a time use inventory is a good way to start. A time use inventory is a list of ways your time is spent.

From your priority chart, schedule the time for things you want to do. Write each one on your time use inventory. Fill in the entire 24-hour period. You will not use every item on your priority chart every day. Some things will be done every day. Others will be done once or twice a week. The important thing is to plan ahead and schedule time for your priorities.

Take the time use inventory with you. Cross off activities once they are completed. If you don't finish a job scheduled for today, move it to your inventory for tomorrow. If you do not have time to finish, look for items you can eliminate. See if you can combine two activities, like folding clothes and talking on the phone.

Rose Anna knew she was wasting time on the telephone and watching TV in the evenings. Every morning she rushed to get to work. At night she was too tired to study the manual for the supervisor's position. She made a plan to use her time more carefully. Rose Anna's time use inventory for one day is shown here, in Illustration 3-3.

Time Use Inventory

6 a.m.	Get up; exercise. 6:30: Dress; fix breakfast.	6 p.m.	Pick up Tisha. Back home— Watch TV.
7	Breakfast with Buster & Tisha. Clean kitchen.	7	Fix dinner. Dinner with Tisha & Buster.
8	Get Buster off to school. Take Tisha to daycare.	8	Read to Tisha; put her to bed. Help Buster with homework.
9	Work.	9	Fix Buster's Lunch for tomorrow. Lay out clothes. Fill in daily expense log.
10	"	10	Fill out tomorrow's time use inventory. Watch some TV.
11	"	11	Get ready for bed.
12	Lunch with Vera. 12:30: Study supervisor's manual	12	Sleep.
1	Back to work.	1	"
2	Break— 2:45: visit with Vera & Jerry.	2	"
3	Work.	3	"
4	"	4	"
5	"	5	"

Illustration 3-3

Rose Anna's Time Use Inventory

CHECKPOINT 3-3

YOUR GOAL: Get 22 or more points.

Prepare a time use inventory for yourself. Use the form below to make a plan for Monday. Include setting a time to work on several of the priorities you listed in Checkpoint 3-2. Fill in every hour of the day, including the time you will sleep. A good example for everyone is listed at 8:00 p.m.

Time Use Inventory

6 AM	______	6 PM	______
7	______	7	______
8	______	8	*Prepare tomorrow's time use inventory.*
9	______	9	______
10	______	10	______
11	______	11	______
12	______	12	______
1	______	1	______
2	______	2	______
3	______	3	______
4	______	4	______
5	______	5	______

☞ *Check your work on page 54. Record your score on page 58.*

SAVING MONEY

Managing your money includes saving money. Before you make a saving plan, check out your present finances. If you are in debt, get out of debt and learn to live on less.

Danger Signals

Before you can begin to save, you may need to get out of debt. Here are some danger signals that indicate you are headed for financial trouble. Ask yourself if any of these signals apply to you:

1. You owe more than seven people or businesses.
2. You depend on extra jobs to make ends meet.
3. You get behind in rent or utility payments.
4. You have less than two months' take-home pay set aside in cash or savings.
5. You don't know how much your monthly expenses are.
6. You don't know how much your total debt is.
7. You have back bills that will take more than 12 months to repay.
8. You are using savings to pay monthly expenses.

Steps to Getting Out of Financial Trouble

If you answered yes to three or more of these questions, you may be headed for financial trouble. Here are steps to follow to help you get out of trouble:

1. Make a list of everyone you owe.
2. Decide how much you can pay back each month.
3. Make a plan to start paying those you owe. Your plan should list the most important debts first. For example, back rent or utility bills should be paid off before repaying the $10 you borrowed from a friend. Include dates debts will be paid.
4. Talk to those you owe. Most businesses will cooperate with you if they know you have a plan and are trying to pay off overdue bills.
5. Follow your plan. Keep a copy of your budget and your plan where you can see it. Control your spending carefully so nothing keeps you from making payments on overdue bills.

6. Get help. Nonprofit counseling is available from many colleges and universities, housing authorities, and credit unions. Consumer Credit Counseling Services (CCCS) is a nonprofit organization with local offices in most major cities. Counseling services are free. You can call the number listed in your telephone book and make an appointment.

MAKING YOUR MONEY WORK FOR YOU

The first step to saving time and money is self-control. Try a self-control game with yourself. Pick one habit (such as, buying a soft drink on your afternoon break) and change it for one week. At the end of the week, you will have won the game!

Living on Less

To get out of financial trouble, or to begin saving for the future, you may need to begin living on less. There are other times when living on less is necessary. A family wage earner may lose a job. Unexpected bills may have to be paid. Or you may want to save for a special purchase.

Living on less simply means choosing where cuts can and must be made. To make cuts, first make a list of budget items. Then decide which items can be reduced or eliminated. Rose Anna's neighbor, Harold, got laid off from his job. Harold's take-home pay was $1,400 a month. His unemployment pay was $900 a month. Harold made a plan to help him live on less. He could not reduce his rent payment, but he cut other items. Harold used the bus less and spent less at the grocery store. He also cut down on water and electricity use. Harold's plan is shown on the next page in Illustration 3-4.

Saving for the Future

You can begin saving for the future with $1 or with $100. The important thing is to start now! There are two important words to remember when you start saving:

1. **Principal** is the amount of dollars you save. If you put $10 into a savings account, that $10 is your *principal* amount.
2. **Interest** is the amount your money will earn. The bank or other agency pays for the use of your money. If you invest $10 in a savings account that pays 5 percent interest each year, at the end of the year you will have $10.50 total. Your *principal* is $10.00. Your *interest* is $0.50.

LIVING ON LESS

Income	Column A **Before Reduced Income Amount**	Column B **After Reduced Income Amount**
Salary, wages, earnings	*$1,400*	$
Unemployment compensation		*$ 900*
Child support, alimony		
Salary and tips		
Other		
Total Monthly Income	*$1,400*	*$ 900*
Expenses		
Housing	$ *450*	$ *450*
Utilities	*200*	*150*
Food	*400*	*200*
Transportation	*100*	*50*
Clothing and personal care	*100*	*50*
Medical and health	*50*	
Recreation/ entertainment	*50*	
Savings	*50*	
Other		
Total Monthly Expenses	*$1,400*	*$ 900*

Illustration 3-4

Harold's Plan for Living on Less

Saving Plans

When you begin to save money, you want to make sure your money is safe. You also want your money to earn interest. Three good ways to begin saving are passbook savings accounts, savings clubs, and government savings bonds. Each of these methods will earn interest of about 5 percent to 7 percent per year.

Each of these savings also has good liquidity. **Liquidity** is the ease with which you can get your cash back.

Passbook savings accounts can be opened with a small amount of money at a bank or savings and loan association. A passbook savings account has the advantage of high liquidity. You can get your cash out very quickly if you need it.

Savings clubs, such as a Christmas Club, are available at many banks and other institutions. You make regular payments into the account and agree not to withdraw the money until a certain time. Savings club accounts are not as liquid as passbook savings but are a good way to force yourself to save.

Government savings bonds may be redeemed after six months. Redeem means to get your money back. But savings bonds do not pay interest until the maturity date. The **maturity date** is the date on which you must renew a bond or certificate or cash it in. The average maturity date for a savings bond is between five and ten years from the date of purchase. Savings bonds may be purchased at banks and other institutions.

You can begin saving for the future with $1 or with $100. The important thing is to start now!

CHECKPOINT 3-4

YOUR GOAL: Get 4 or more points.

Read carefully the statements below. Complete each statement by choosing the correct word or words. Write the correct answer in the space provided. An example is done for you.

two months' ______ • One financial danger signal is having less than (two months'/nine months') set aside in cash or savings.

______ 1. Another financial danger signal is owing (more/less) than 7 persons or businesses.

______ 2. (Talking/Not talking) to those you owe is a good step toward getting out of financial trouble.

_______________ 3. It is important to pay (utility bills/personal bills) first.

_______________ 4. Consumer Credit Counseling Services is a (very expensive/free) service to help you get out of debt.

_______________ 5. You (should/should not) use savings to pay monthly expenses.

_______________ 6. If you put money into a passbook savings account, it (will/will not) earn interest.

_______________ 7. Savings club accounts (are/are not) as liquid as passbook accounts.

_______________ 8. Government savings bonds pay interest (immediately/upon maturity).

☞ ***Check your work on page 55. Record your score on page 58.***

WHAT YOU HAVE LEARNED

After studying this unit, you have learned:

- Five obstacles to saving time.
- To set priorities for time use.
- To prepare a time use inventory.
- Five steps toward getting out of financial trouble.
- Two ways to save for the future.

PUTTING IT TOGETHER

ACTIVITY 3-1 YOUR GOAL: Get 5 or more points.

Match the obstacle to using time wisely in the first column with the action that overcomes that obstacle in the second column. Write your answer in the space provided. An example is done for you.

Obstacle

f ● Putting things off.

____ 1. Being too tired.

____ 2. Failure to plan.

____ 3. Telephone calls.

____ 4. Television.

____ 5. Mail.

____ 6. Doing jobs in the wrong order.

____ 7. Clutter.

Action to Overcome Obstacle

a. Stand up when you talk on the telephone.

b. Limit your TV time.

c. Don't try to do all your big jobs on one day.

d. Make a list of activities you need to do.

e. Keep your work area clean.

f. Do it now.

g. Do the most difficult one first.

h. Put the bills where you can pay them without looking for them.

☞ *Check your work on page 55. Record your score on page 58.*

ACTIVITY 3-2 YOUR GOAL: Get 8 or more points.

Assume that you were laid off from a part-time job which paid $400 take-home pay per month. How would you change your budget items shown on the following page? Assume that your full-time employment gives you take-home pay of $1,000 per month. Write your answers in the space provided in Column B. Column A is done for you.

LIVING ON LESS

Income		
Salary, wages, earnings	$1,000	$1,000
Unemployment compensation		
Child support, alimony		
Salary and tips	400	----
Other		
Total Monthly Income	1,400	
Expenses		
Housing	325	
Utilities	75	
Food	300	
Transportation	140	
Clothing and personal care	140	
Medical and health	80	
Recreation/ entertainment	200	
Savings	70	
Other	70	
Total Monthly Expenses	$1,400	

☞ ***Check your work on page 55. Record your score on page 58.***

Activity 3-3 YOUR GOAL: Get 8 or more points.

Identify each statement below by choosing *a, b,* or *c.* Write your answer in the space provided. An example is done for you.

a. a danger signal
b. a step to getting out of financial trouble
c. a savings plan

a • You get behind in rent or utility payments.

_____ 1. Make a list of everyone you owe.

_____ 2. You owe more than seven people or businesses.

_____ 3. You can open a passbook savings account with a small amount of money.

_____ 4. Talk to those you owe.

_____ 5. Consumer Credit Counseling Services is a nonprofit organization whose services are free.

_____ 6. You depend on extra jobs to make ends meet.

_____ 7. Make a plan listing the most important debts first.

_____ 8. Make regular payment into a Christmas Club account.

_____ 9. Keep a copy of your budget and your plan where you can see it.

_____ 10. You don't know how much your total debt is.

☞ ***Check your work on page 55. Record your score on page 58.***

CHECKING WHAT YOU LEARNED

Now you can see how much you have learned about budgeting your time and money. These 20 questions cover the main topics you studied in this book. There is no time limit, so take your time.

After you finish, check your answers. Give yourself 1 point for each correct answer. Record your score on your Personal Progress Record. The evaluation chart will tell you where you may need additional study.

DIRECTIONS: Each statement is either true or false. Write *T* (true) or *F* (false) in the space provided.

______ 1. Income is the amount of money paid to you during a period of time.

______ 2. Net pay is the amount left after all deductions have been taken out of your paycheck.

______ 3. Child support is money paid by the government to a parent.

______ 4. Expenses are receipts for gifts and services.

______ 5. A budget is a written plan to help you live within your income.

______ 6. A daily log is a record of money spent each day.

______ 7. Some income and expenses do not need to be included in a budget.

______ 8. You will save money on your electric bill if you let the sun shine through the windows in winter.

______ 9. It costs the same to telephone from Chicago to Miami every day of the week.

______ 10. Unit pricing is a gimmick used by stores to trick you into buying more than you should.

______ 11. Buying goods out of season can help cut costs.

______ 12. Comparison shopping is a waste of time.

______ 13. Advertisers and sellers count on impulse buyers to boost sales.

______ 14. You can control your variable expenses.

______ 15. Standing up while talking on the phone helps save time because you don't talk as long.

______ 16. Writing down a time use inventory every day is a waste of time.

______ 17. Priorities are orders of importance.

______ 18. Once you make a priority chart, it will always stay the same.

______ 19. You may be headed for financial trouble if you depend on extra jobs to make ends meet.

______ 20. You must have at least $100 to open a passbook savings account.

☞ ***Check your work on page 55. Record your score on page 59.***

GLOSSARY

A

Aid to Families with Dependent Children (AFDC). Money paid by the federal government to low-income families with dependent children.

B

Budget. A written plan to help you live within your income.

C

Child support. Money paid by one parent to the other for the support of dependent children.

D

Decimal amount. A number using a decimal point (period) to show the percentage.

Dependent. Someone who relies on another for support.

E

Expenses. Payments for goods and services.

F

Fixed expenses. Expenses that are the same every month.

G

Gross pay. The total amount of earnings for a specified period of time such as one month, two weeks, or one week.

I

Impulse buying. Spending money suddenly for something because you think you want it.

Income. The amount of money paid to you during a period of time.

Interest. The amount your money will earn. The amount paid for the use of capital.

L

Liquidity. The ease with which you can get your cash back.

M

Maturity date. The date on which you must renew a bond or certificate or cash it in.

N

Net pay. The amount of take-home pay you receive, after all the deductions are taken out of your gross pay.

O

Obstacle. Something that stands in your way.

P

Percentages. Fractions using 100 to represent the whole.

Principal. The amount of dollars you save.

Priorities. Orders of importance.

U

Unit pricing. Showing the price of an item by one unit: by weight, quantity, or piece.

V

Variable expenses. Expenses that vary from day to day.

INDEX

ANSWERS

✔ CHECKING WHAT YOU KNOW

1. **T**	9. **T**	15. **T**
2. **T**	10. **T**	16. **F**
3. **F**	11. **F**	17. **T**
4. **T**	12. **T**	18. **T**
5. **T**	13. **F**	19. **T**
6. **T**	14. **F**	20. **F**
7. **F**		
8. **F**		

UNIT 1

CHECKPOINT 1-1, page 5

Give yourself 1 point for each source of income and the amount listed. Give yourself 1 point for the correct total amount.

CHECKPOINT 1-2, page 6

Give yourself 1 point for each fixed expense and the amount listed. Give yourself 1 point for the correct total amount of fixed expenses.

CHECKPOINT 1-3, page 8

Give yourself 1 point for each variable expense listed. Check the amounts. Give yourself 1 point for the correct total amount of variable expenses.

CHECKPOINT 1-4, page 10

Give yourself 1 point for writing what you spent each day for one week. Give yourself 1 point for writing the weekly totals in the eighth section of your log.

ACTIVITY 1-1, page 13

Give yourself 1 point for filling in each item and each total in the budget form with your own amounts.

ACTIVITY 1-2, page 14

Check below and give yourself 1 point for writing each day's expenses correctly. Give yourself 1 point for each overspent item correctly identified and circled.

Monday	***Tuesday***	***Wednesday***	***Thursday***
Groceries, $20 *Lunch 5*	*Personal items $10* *Lunch 10* *Movies 14*	*Lunch $10*	*Groceries $40* *Lunch 5* *Movies 14*
Friday	***Saturday***	***Sunday***	***TOTALS***
Personal items $16 *Lunch 10* *Clothing 5*	*Groceries $10* *Clothing 10* *Movies 7*	*Personal items $5*	*Groceries $70* *Lunch 40* *Personal items 31* *Movies 35* *Clothing 15*

UNIT 2

CHECKPOINT 2-1, page 20

Give yourself 1 point for each correct answer.

1. **F**
2. **T**
3. **T**
4. **F**
5. **T**
6. **F**

CHECKPOINT 2-2, page 22

Give yourself 1 point for each correct answer.

1. **$600**
2. **$120**
3. **$240**
4. **$120**
5. **$240**
6. **$120**
7. **$240**
8. **$120**

CHECKPOINT 2-3, page 26

Give yourself 1 point for each correct answer.

1. **cold water**
2. **clothes dryer**
3. **directory assistance**
4. **unit price**
5. **leaky faucets**
6. **thermostat**

ACTIVITY 2-1, page 27

More than one choice may apply to each circumstance. Give yourself 1 point for each question and each rule written.

1. Question: **Can I postpone buying it for one week and see if I still need it then?**

Rule: **Substitute. Look for something else that will work just as well for less.**

2. Question: **Can I postpone buying it and save credit costs?**

Rule: **Compare. Check the same item at two or more stores to find the best buy.**

3. Question: **Am I being taken in by advertising?**

Rule: **Ask questions. Don't believe everything the ads say.**

4. Question: **Can I buy it later, maybe when it is on sale?**

Rule: **Shop around. Watch for sales.**

5. Question: **Can I make it myself and save money?**

Rule: **Do it yourself. Buy used goods and refinish them.**

ACTIVITY 2-2, page 28

More than one correct choice may apply to each action. Give yourself 1 point for each saving identified.

1. **a**
2. **b**
3. **e**
4. **a** (or **c**)
5. **b**
6. **c** (or **a**)

ACTIVITY 2-3, page 29

Give yourself 1 point for each correct answer.

1. **c**
2. **b**
3. **a**
4. **b**
5. **a**

UNIT 3

CHECKPOINT 3-1, page 32

Give yourself 1 point for each correct answer.

1. **T**
2. **F**
3. **T**
4. **T**
5. **F**
6. **T**

CHECKPOINT 3-2, page 34

Give yourself 1 point for each activity listed. Answers will vary.

CHECKPOINT 3-3, page 37

Give yourself 1 point for each hour where you have listed at least one activity. Answers will vary.

CHECKPOINT 3-4, page 41

Give yourself 1 point for each correct answer.

1. **more**
2. **Talking**
3. **utility bills**
4. **free**
5. **should not**
6. **will**
7. **are not**
8. **upon maturity**

ACTIVITY 3-1, page 43

Give yourself 1 point for each correct answer.

1. **c**
2. **d**
3. **a**
4. **b**
5. **h**
6. **g**
7. **e**

ACTIVITY 3-2, page 43

Give yourself 10 points for completing Column B. Deduct 2 points if the total of Column B is not $1,000. Answers will vary as each student determines where he or she would reduce expenses. However, the total of the expenses in Column B should be $1,000.

ACTIVITY 3-3, page 45

Give yourself 1 point for each correct answer.

1. **b**
2. **a**
3. **c**
4. **b**
5. **b**
6. **a**
7. **b**
8. **c**
9. **b**
10. **a**

✔ CHECKING WHAT YOU LEARNED

1. **T**
2. **T**
3. **F**
4. **F**
5. **T**
6. **F**
7. **F**
8. **T**
9. **F**
10. **F**
11. **T**
12. **F**
13. **T**
14. **T**
15. **T**
16. **F**
17. **T**
18. **F**
19. **T**
20. **F**

PERSONAL PROGRESS RECORD

Name: ______________________________

✔ CHECKING WHAT YOU KNOW

Use the chart below to determine the areas you need to do the most work. In the space provided, write the total number of points you got right for each content area. Then add up the total number of points right to find your final score. Circle those items you answered correcly. As you begin your study, pay close attention to those areas where you missed half or more of the questions.

Content Area	Item Number	Study Pages	Total Points	Number Right
UNIT 1				
Income	1, 2, 3	2-4	3	
Expenses	4, 6	5-9	2	
Monthly Budget	5, 7	10-11	2	
Unit 2				
Controlling Variable Expenses	8, 14	17-20	2	
Tips for Cutting Costs	9, 10, 11	23-25	5	
Unit 3				
Saving Time	15, 16, 17	31-37	3	
Saving Money	18, 19, 20	38-41	3	

Date ______________________ Total Points: 20 Your Score: ______

UNIT 1: Using a Budget

Exercise	Score
Checkpoint 1-1	______
Checkpoint 1-2	______
Checkpoint 1-3	______
Checkpoint 1-4	______
Activity 1-1	______
Activity 1-2	______
Total	______

HOW ARE YOU DOING?

28 or better	**Excellent**
23-27	**Good**
18-22	**Fair**
Less than 18	**See Instructor**

UNIT 2: Cutting Costs

Exercise	Score
Checkpoint 2-1	______
Checkpoint 2-2	______
Checkpoint 2-3	______
Activity 2-1	______
Activity 2-2	______
Activity 2-3	______
Total	______

HOW ARE YOU DOING?

28 or better	**Excellent**
24-27	**Good**
20-23	**Fair**
Less than 20	**See Instructor**

UNIT 3: Saving Time and Money

Exercise	Score
Checkpoint 3-1	______
Checkpoint 3-2	______
Checkpoint 3-3	______
Checkpoint 3-4	______
Activity 3-1	______
Activity 3-2	______
Activity 3-3	______
Total	______

HOW ARE YOU DOING?

61 or better	**Excellent**
56-60	**Good**
51-55	**Fair**
Less than 51	**See Instructor**

Name: ______________________________

✔ CHECKING WHAT YOU LEARNED

Use the chart below to determine the areas you need to do the most review. In the space provided, write the total number of points you got right for each content area. Review those areas where you missed half or more of the questions. Then add up the total number of points right to find your final score.

Content Area	Item Number	Study Pages	Total Points	Number Right
UNIT 1				
Income	1, 2, 3	2-4	3	
Expenses	4, 6	5-9	2	
Monthly Budget	5, 7	10-11	2	
Unit 2				
Controlling Variable Expenses	11, 12, 13, 14	17-20	4	
Tips for Cutting Costs	8, 9, 10	23-25	3	
Unit 3				
Saving Time	15, 16, 17, 18	31-37	4	
Saving Money	19, 20	38-41	2	

Date ______________________ Total Points: 20 Your Score: ____